HIGH COLOR

HIGH COLOR

SPECTACULAR
WILDFLOWERS
of the
ROCKIES

Photography
by
Linde Waidhofer

Text by
Lito Tejada-Flores

WESTERN EYE PRESS

Dandelions in May, Wilson Peak, Colorado

Spring stumbles helter skelter into these high Rockies, long before winter gives up its white ghost. Snowfields retreat step by step toward the safety of rocky summits. The ragtag advance of early spring color pushes on and up, through foothills into the front ranges, over low passes into the high country. Every year this same alpine rough and tumble rages across fairy meadows, first flowers versus last snow. Every year the battle is won in advance. Every year color defeats monochrome. High color coming home.

It's more than change, it's revolution. And the humblest flowers, little more than weeds, play the biggest role. The least are, for once, the first. Dandelions fight the good fight; liberate the high country from winter's hold; carpet the hills in yellow-on-yellow brocade before finer flowers even pull themselves upright. But they're only the vanguard. A rainbow of early flowers fills in the ranks behind them. Winter fades like a white dream and the Rockies wake up, awash in floral sunshine.

Early Dandelions

Dandelions, abandoned sheep ranch

Pasque Flowers

Pasque Flower a few weeks later

Silvery Lupine and Paintbrush

Silvery Lupine among Mule's Ears

Every year, first flowers work their strong medicine on the mind, on the heart, in a way that's totally predictable, totally surprising. Each new color added to the high mountain palate affects me in a way that the showiest blossoms of July and August never quite equal.

The first whites: tiny globes of Marsh Marigold bubbling up out of marsh and mud. The first blues: an architecture of Lupine stalks on dry south-facing hillsides. The first reds: a rash of Paintbrush in open fields and tiny flames of Crimson Columbine under the aspens. I rush home with the news. Guess what I saw today, come, come and look. . . .

In real life, by definition, firsts come only once. But in the high Rockies, as if by special dispensation, such logic doesn't seem to apply. Like a mountain climber, spring color works its way slowly uphill, one valley, one bench, one life zone at a time. So the heart-stopping beauty of first flowers is repeated over and over, at ever higher altitudes.

In a real sense there is no spring in the Rockies not as a separate season anyway — although you can find it here and there, lower or higher or higher still, week by week. Spring is the floating moment of transition between snow and sun, between winter cold and summer warmth that sweeps through these mountains, opening doors, and is gone. The transition to alpine summer, a season of desperate, joyous, high-speed growth, is seamless and swift. First flowers are the heroes of this revolution and in the fashion of heroes, they disappear quickly.

11

Crimson Columbine

Crimson Columbine

Mule's Ears, southern Colorado

Mule's Ears detail

Wild Bergamont

Bristle Thistle

First Glacier Lilies, Cascade Canyon, Teton National Park, Wyoming

Glacier Lilies

Glacier Lilies

Glacier Lilies, Glacier National Park, Montana

Western Wood Lilies

Western Wood Lily detail

Prairie Smoke

Prairie Smoke after blooming

Paintbrush and Lowbush Penstemon, Glacier National Park, Montana

Ten years ago I moved to the Rocky Mountains, already a rock climber and mountaineer, full of enthusiasm, full of misconceptions. Mountains, I already knew, were hard and harsh — sterile, stately kingdoms of granite and snow with gnarled windblasted trees, with grasses and flowers that struggled rather than flourished. A range called the Rocky Mountains could hardly be otherwise. Right? Wrong.

At first it was the landscape itself that seemed wrong. Mountain grasses, I knew, are not supposed to grow almost to the summit of 14,000 foot peaks. In the Rockies they do. High mountain forests, I knew, are not supposed to tremble and dance on windless days, burst into flame each autumn, rise limegreen and glistening from the wreckage each spring. In the Rockies they do. Mountain flowers, I knew, are meant to be scattered, unlikely exceptions, rare glimpses of hard-to-find color in a landscape of somber tones and deep hues, of mineral grey, sky blue, and pineneedle green. Not so in the Rockies.

These mountains are colored like no others. From red dirt crags that first suggested the name *Colorado* to the Spaniards, to the eyedazzling turquoise of glacial lakes in the Canadian Rockies, color is everywhere. But in wildflowers, Rocky Mountain color reaches a kind of critical mass and ignites, explodes across the steep landscape like a firestorm, a summerlong burst of unrestrained beauty.

For the first time in my life I became obsessed with flowers. Suddenly I had to learn all their names as if, by poring over field guides, I might understand the secret of their wild profusion. Alpine flowers dot all the memories of my first climbs in the Rockies; fellwalking along grand green sweeps of high tundra seemed only an excuse to discover more flowers; and somehow all these new ranges were translated into new combinations and recombinations of color.

My first summer in the Rockies passed like a green and flowered dream. And I haven't gotten over it yet.

Sticky Purple Geranium and Mountain Meadow Cinquefoil

A forest fantasy: Paintbrush, Mountain Bluebell, Arnica,
Arrowleaf Ragwort, Sticky Geranium and Tall Purple Fleabane

29

Tall Purple Fleabane

Oxeye Daisies

Tall Purple Fleabane, Scarlet Paintbrush, Groundsel and Wild Buckwheat

Scarlet Paintbrush, Groundsel, Wild Buckwheat and Wild Chives

Yellow Lady's Slipper, Yoho National Park, Canada

F or heaven's sakes be careful, or you'll crush them!" Linde drops to all fours, advances on hands and knees across the forest floor, sun-puddled and shadow-hatched, a tangle of deadfall and broken bark, mushrooms and moss. "Look there! No bigger than my fingernail."

It's true, these treasures of the forest floor are so small you could walk by them for years, walk right over them, without a second glance. I did. We both did. Until Linde's inquisitive camera aroused the instincts of a floral detective, and we began to search for Rocky Mountain orchids. Orchids? At 10,000 feet? Under the shadow of massive north walls? Along the shady, wet banks of lichen-green alpine lakes? Under branching vaults of Englemann spruce and white fir? Yes, orchids, real orchids, in miniature.

These small and magical gems are quite the other end of the spectrum from the madcap, psychedelic riot of color that Rocky Mountain wildflowers usually spread across open meadows, on sunny south slopes. A discreet beauty hiding behind fallen logs. Easy enough to appreciate, devilishly hard to find. We took nearly ten years to find our first Calypso Orchid in Colorado; yet in Canada we wandered out looking for moose at a salt seep one morning, and stumbled by accident into a swamp full of yellow Lady's Slippers. Flowers this small do more than delight one's vision, they sharpen it. Shadowy forest bogs will never be the same now. Neither will we.

Orchids, of numerous species, though anything but numerous in the Rockies today, aren't the only micro prizes of the forest floor. Twin flowers bloom in colorless Zen-like simplicity, dwarfed by dwarf pine cones. Shooting stars shoot magenta sparks upward from the level of boot laces. High color underfoot.

Fairy Slipper, Colorado

Spotted Orchid, Emerald Lake, British Columbia

Shooting Stars

Twin Flowers

Dwarf Dogwood

Yellow Columbine

Yellow Columbine beneath the Grand Teton, Wyoming

43

M idsummer arrives in the high country wrapped in rainbows after each and every afternoon thundershower; smelling of fir needles, wild onions, and mint; sunburned and peeling under a high-altitude sun. Midsummer in the Rockies surprises you with the sheer number, the veritable excess of its wildflowers. More this week than last, and even more next week in fields that you'd swear couldn't hold another blossom. Where, when, you wonder, does this explosion of color slow down? It doesn't.

The last lumpy avalanche debris melts out of creekbeds and gullies. A few final scraps of snow cling like memories to the north slopes of the highest summits. The early intensity of aspen leaves has dulled to a dark listless green, trembling patiently toward a distant autumn in seemingly motionless air. Warm afternoons stretch to infinity in all directions across flowered meadows.

Marmots bask on their rock castles, forgetting the endless scurry for food, staring motionless at a sea of wildflowers. What do they really see? Cowboys who've driven their cattle up into the high country for summer pasture lie on their backs in bright meadows and roll smokes or chew Copenhagen. Their horses graze on a rich mix of 50% grass, 50% flowers. Spanish and Navajo sheepherders stomp up the high valleys of their National Forest grazing areas. Shouting, waving their hats and whistling to their dogs, they run through clouds of Columbine, Larkspur, Penstemon and Sticky Geranium to push their idiot flocks away from cliffs and back toward good grazing.

Summer in the Rockies with its hot summer colors: damn near washed out in so much sunlight. A lazy, sleepy time, all battles won and winter far away. Flowers everywhere, as if they owned these mountains. Don't they? In the most improbable combinations, as if all colors go perfectly together. Don't they? As if so much beauty was simply in the natural order of things, was inevitable. Isn't it?

Yellow Columbine, Marmot

45

Shortstyle Wild Onion, Bridger/Teton National Forest, Wyoming

Shortstyle Wild Onion detail

Skyrocket and Tall One-sided Penstemon, western Colorado

Skyrocket and Penstemon detail

Orange Sneezeweed, Arnica, Paintbrush, Wild Buckwheat and Sticky Geranium

Fireweed

Fireweed beneath the Maroon Bells, Colorado

Fireweed

Blue Columbine, Colorado

Blue Columbine and Giant Red Paintbrush

Paintbrush

P ainted landscapes. The West is chock full of painted this, and painted that. One county boasts a "painted canyon," another a "painted butte." There are "painted deserts" and "painted rocks." "Paint pots" bubble in mud flats and hot springs from Yellowstone to Kootenay. But in all this color smeared, or better "brushed," across the western landscape, nowhere is the word paint better applied than to the ubiquitous Paintbrush.

Nineteenth century romantics would have called these small, intense members of the *Castilleja* clan "noble blossoms;" and often did, writing descriptions of western wildflowers in a prose so purple it makes us blush. Their extravagant expressions no longer form easily in our matter-of-fact modern mouths. But the feeling persists.

The hills are still colored with Paintbrush, more varieties of Paintbrush than the weekend botanist can possibly cope with, in more shapes and more hues, in a wider, wilder palate than any other flower in these Rocky Mountains. No minimalism, no restraint here. Paintbrushes dot the Rockies with an alarming brilliance: a pointillist fantasy that respects neither contour lines nor life zones. Paintbrush are everywhere, low and high, dry or wet, spreading their almost iridescent pigment, their message of color, their chromatic good cheer.

I stumble over a ridgeline at 13,000 feet, throw my heavy pack off, and flop down on the short tundra grass on the lee side. Looking out, I see past a couple of fourteeners, El Diente and Mount Wilson, all the way out to the Canyonland country of Utah. My gaze falls back to the grass below me, dropping out of sight to end in hidden cliffs. Everywhere around me the sulphur-yellow flames of Lemon Paintbrush, hundreds of them. Even here.

Down we tumble from timberline into the swampy bottom of Cascade Canyon beneath the Grand Teton and Mount Owen, and suddenly find that Crimson Paintbrush have thrown a blood-red roadblock across the trail. Here too.

Evening sneaks softly down the last sandy canyons where the main Rockies merge westward into high desert. Chaparral, sage and cactus, twisted juniper and fragrant piñon tempt us out of our mountains into another world. Even here, spikey orange Paintbrush catch the last sun, glow like coals. Here too. Everywhere.

Giant Red Paintbrush

Paintbrush and Wild Chives

Desert Paintbrush

Lemon Paintbrush

Yellow Monkey Flower

Elephant's Head

Orange Sneezeweed, Sticky Geranium and Paintbrush

The morning meadow still wet with dew. Grass, rushes and sedges send up puffs of steam, baking dry in the clear lemon-yellow August sunshine. The deer have been out nibbling at the salty tree trunk below our cabin since dawn; they browse slowly downslope toward forest's edge, shade and shelter, tree dark, leaf cool. I count antlers, then heads — one's missing — and set off to fell a dead tree for firewood. Lugging my greasy McCullough chainsaw though waistdeep drifts of flowers. Mountain Bluebells, tangles of them, bunches, bushes full, even though they don't exactly grow on bushes. Crimson Paintbrush and rusty King's Crown for contrast. Showy Fleabane making a comeback where we burned brush last summer. But above all Bluebells. This morning, this meadow, belongs to the Bluebells — half of them more pinkish than blue — scattered in a high haze above the green. I plow on, feeling like a summer tourist at the beach, wading out through the surf for the first time. Surprised. Delighted. Unbelieving.

   Pushing through a particularly dense thicket, I almost trip over the missing deer. Youngest of the band, a fawn still covered in spots, curled asleep in a child's fort of Bluebells. Too drowsy to bolt, it wakes slowly, moves slowly away, downslope like the others, into the forest. I shake my head and stare at the crushed bed of flowers at my feet to prove it really happened. Surprised. Delighted. Unbelieving.

Mountain Harebell with Butter and Eggs

Mountain Harebell

Mariposa Lilies

Mariposa Lilies

Butterweed Groundsel beneath the Tetons, Grand Teton National Park, Wyoming

Mule's Ears under the Tetons

C omes a moment, high in the high Rockies, when wildflowers are no longer intruders, newcomers, colored fragments of another reality. They become reality itself.

Comes a moment when mountain meadows are no longer open acres of green silk dotted with occasional blooms, but solid carpets of solid color where the inquisitive eye can still pick out a few blades, tufts, patches of grass, scattered here and there through a universe of wildflowers.

Comes a last, lightheaded moment when you give yourself over completely to the charm of intense color. Wall to wall color, horizon to horizon color, sky to earth color.

Late summer meadows are the primitive prototypes of modern color field painting. No graphic artist would dare dispense pigment with such a lavish hand. No tribal nomad, crosslegged before a loom in wild lost landscape, would dare weave tapestries of such pure color. These broad wildflower tapestries challenge the senses, stir the emotions and defy reason. Wildflowers, a small common-sense voice inside me whispers, are quite spectacular enough, thank you! in ones and twos, in small discrete bunches. There's no reason they should try to take over the world. And yet they do.

The cumulative effect of hundreds, thousands, tens of thousands of flowers, changes the viewer even more than the landscape. You become not merely used to such beauty, but dependent on it. No two fields are ever the same; and once you've gotten over your initial surprise at dense flower carpets stretching out of sight, the very notion, the thought of mountain flowers will never be the same either. Wildflower tapestries build slowly to a late summer crescendo: high color at its highest saturation. . . .

Colorado Loco, Tall One-sided Penstemon and Paintbrush

Shortstyle Wild Onion and Mountain Meadow Cinquefoil

Paintbrush, Cinquefoil, Sticky Geranium and Sedges

Green Gentian

Big Mountain or Blue Gentian

Bear Grass, Paintbrush and Tall Purple Fleabane, Glacier National Park, Montana

Chainpod

S nowing! Snowing in July! Well, this isn't exactly a classic snowfall. These are not the lacy, featherlight, six-sided crystals skiers dream of, but hard pelletlike dots of windborne ice. Snow that stings the face, pounds the rough boulders of a sprawling ridgeline above 14,000 feet, covers the high tundra blossoms in a second skin of granular white. Happens all the time up here on the roof of the continent.

Half an hour later the squall has passed; high winds are tearing the last clouds to shreds; mist curtains in the valleys below open and shut, revealing then hiding dark forests, pools of shadow that must be lakes. Up here on the high alpine tundra, sun and wind are both busy, freeing a strange community of flowers from their temporary blanket of summer snow.

Tundra flowers are more than strange; they are improbable, unlikely, just plain out of place. These are dwarf flowers, massed in ground-hugging mats, magnificently adapted to one of the harshest environments on the planet. Many of the high alpine tundra flowers of the Rockies are cousins, or twins, of wildflowers that bloom only in the arctic. There isn't that much difference between the two environments except, of course, that up here on the Continental Divide the air is far thinner, and summer actually shorter.

In the few short weeks of real summer above timberline, a floral alchemy transforms these barren fell fields, ridges and draws. They aren't barren at all, but you have to search out the patches of green, the hidden gardens wedged in the shelter of tumbled blocks, the low pillows of Moss Pink, Alpine Forget-me-nots and white Flox. Like detectives we comb through boulderfields looking for a perfect circle of white blossoms, Spring Beauty, a succulent that blooms long after spring has come and gone in the real world down below. In the unreal world of high color, these microflowers of the tundra are surely the most unexpected and incongruous of wildflowers. The highest color of all.

Sky Pilot

Spotted Saxifrage

Pink Moss Campion and Whiplash Saxifrage

Spring Beauty with Dwarf Clover and Pussy Toes

Dwarf Clover

Blue Columbine

Paintbrush and Queen Anne's Lace

Everyone has a special place, a locus of power and attachment. And every wildflower lover has a secret (or not so secret) valley, creekside or field that outshines all the rest. A place with more, brighter, bigger, or simply subtler flowers that you return to summer after summer. A mountain flower garden that astonishes you just as much after five years as the day you first saw it.

For Linde and myself, such a place is Yankee Boy Basin: a high green fold in the San Juans of southwestern Colorado, scarred with the tailings piles and glory holes of a long past gold-mining boom, redeemed by the richest explosion, the greatest variety of wildflowers we've ever encountered in one valley. We live only a few hours away from this mecca of high color, and every year in July start asking each other: "Do you think Yankee Boy's in bloom yet?" With such impatience, we always get there too early, while the Arizona monsoons are still soaking the alpine grasses, setting the stage for the color to come. Which always comes. Which always leaves us speechless.

Yankee Boy is unique in our lives and, I think, in our corner of the Rockies. But it's hardly unique in the whole of the Rocky Mountains, or in the whole gamut of North American mountain ranges. Our friends in Wyoming, in Montana, have their own extraordinary wildflower stashes. Meadows and valleys so bright with flowers that old timers will tell you stories about them, and rambunctious children fall silent with awe at so much color.

Yet Yankee Boy and its flowers aren't safe. When someone wants to renew the patent on an old mining claim and bulldoze a new road through this magic landscape, they do so with impunity. The enjoyment of wildflowers doesn't seem to be one of the high priority uses that the "Land of Many Uses" signs in our National Forests allude to. Why can't Yankee Boy Basin and other similarly stunning wildflower sites across the Rockies be protected in a series of National Wildflower Preserves? Just because this beauty is so ephemeral — pushing up through the snow to bloom and die again each summer — should we give it less protection than the granite crags and sandstone spires in our great National Parks? Of course not.

In some areas, in some ranges, high color is threatened, diminished, gone. Nineteenth century tourists nearly picked the Alps clean of flowers. We're luckier in the Rockies. But luck alone won't keep our high color from fading. Perhaps enough love and lobbying might.

Blue Columbine, Yankee Boy Basin, Colorado

About the Flowers

As a photographer I love wildflowers for their strange forms, their rich colors. But beauty and botany are not incompatible. Sooner or later, anyone who falls under the spell of high color wants to know more about these magical mountain flowers. The following notes are brief, almost telegraphic jottings about the flowers in this book. For those wishing to delve deeper into the mysteries of family, genus and species, into the fact and folklore of wildflowers, I include a recommended source list.

Linde Waidhofer

2 **Common Dandelion**
4 *Taraxacum officinale*
5 This lowly flower, an escapee from Europe and the scourge of so many lawns, turns the flanks of southern Rockies into an El Dorado in May and early June. San Juan mountains, Colorado.

6 **Pasque Flower**
7 *Pulsatilla patens*
(formerly Anemone patens)
One of the earliest spring flowers. A strange and wonderful transformation turns the flower into a ghostly bundle of wirelike strands after the petals have fallen off. Also called Wild Crocus and Lion's Beard.

8 **Silvery Lupine**
Lupinus argenteus
Paintbrush
Castilleja sp.
Some 50 species of Lupine and False Lupine occur in the Rockies. They're all early bloomers and can turn open meadows among aspen trees a solid blue. They disappear by early July to leave room for the next wave of color.

9 **Silvery Lupine**
Lupinus argenteus
Mule's Ears
Wyethia amplexicaulis
Horizon to horizon flowers on Hastings Mesa beneath the north slopes of the Sneffels Range, Colorado.

10 **Rocky Mountain Iris**
Iris missouriensis
Found in profusion in marshy wetlands around ponds and low-lying mountain lakes. Color ranges from pale white to deep purple. By mid-June they are only a wilted memory.

12 **Crimson Columbine**
13 *Aquilegia elegantula*
This is a small but spectacular cousin of the better known Blue Columbine. The Crimson Columbine is found at lower altitudes, prefers open forests to alpine slopes, and blooms much earlier in the summer.

14 **Mule's Ears**
15 *Wyethia amplexicaulis*
Mule's Ears take up the baton from the Dandelion and keep the high meadows yellow for a few more weeks. These impressive fields are an annual late June happening at 10,000 ft. beneath Hayden Peak, Mears Peak and Mt. Wolcott in the Sneffels Range, Colorado.

16 **Wild Bergamont**
Monarda fistulosa
A member of the mint family, also called Horse Mint, and Mintleaf Beebalm, with a strong minty aroma. Wild Bergamont is rare in much of the Rockies, but can be easily spotted in meadowland around the US/Canadian border. These beauties were photographed in Waterton Lakes National Park, Canada.

17 **Bristle Thistle**
Cirsium undulatam
This member of the sunflower family is an import to the new world but is now found throughout the Rockies. Like many thistles, its blossoms are very showy, and delight the eye once one gets past a natural prejudice against prickly plants.

18 **Glacier Lily**
19 *Erythronium grandiflorum*
20 These lilies follow retreating
21 snowfields up into the highest alpine life zones, often bursting up through the last few centimeters of unmelted snow. Found from Colorado to the Canadian Rockies, they are also called Snow Lily and Avalanche Lily. The same names are often applied to a similar flower, *Erythronium montanum* .

22 **Western Wood Lily**
23 *Lilium philadelphicum*
A spectacular and, in some areas, endangered species. Caution: Wood Lilies grow from bulbs, and picking the flower causes the plant to die! This is probably the rarest flower in Colorado's Rocky Mountain National Park, and hard to find anywhere in the southern Rockies. Less rare in the Canadian parks. Also called Rocky Mountain Lily.

24 **Prairie Smoke**
25 *Erythrocoma triflora*
(formerly Geum Triflorum)
A foothill flower, Prairie Smoke blooms in open meadows. It becomes even more beautiful after it loses its flowers, and the triple stalks straighten up bearing delicate feathery "styles." Sometimes called Old Man's Whiskers.

26 Paintbrush
Castilleja sp.
Lowbush Penstemon
Penstemon fruticosus
Steep hillsides of high color in Glacier National Park, early July. Different species of Penstemon, like Paintbrush, are found everywhere in the Rockies, but this is a northern one, concentrated in Wyoming, Montana, and southern Canada.

28 Sticky Purple Geranium
Geranium viscosissimum
Mountain Meadow Cinquefoil
Potentilla diversifolia
An alpine bouquet, Waterton Lakes National Park, Canada. Sticky Purple Geranium blooms all summer from one end of the Rockies to the other; named for the sticky glandular hairs on branches and stems. Cinquefoil is a member of the Rose family and derives its name from the French, *cinq feuilles*, five leaves or, in this case, five characteristic petals.

29 Sticky Geranium
Geranium richardsonii
Arnica
Arnica sp.
Arrowleaf Ragwort
Senecio triangularis
Mountain Bluebell
Mertensia ciliata
Paintbrush
Castilleja sp.
Tall Purple Fleabane
Erigeron peregrinus
A forest fantasy just below timberline, San Juan mountains, southwestern Colorado. Arrowleaf Groundsel, sometimes called Arrowleaf Ragwort or Giant Ragwort, is found throughout the Rockies. Identify this one by its triangular leaves.

30 Tall Purple Fleabane
Erigeron peregrinus
This flower is often confused with Showy Asters, and is an archetypal example of what most people lump under the general heading of "daisy." Fleabane blooms earlier in the summer than Aster; both are equally lovely.

31 Oxeye Daisy
Leucanthemum vulgare
(formerly Chrysanthemum leucanthemum)
Another member of the Sunflower family, this elegant, simple flower was first introduced from Europe and now grows wild across much of North America and all of the Rockies.

32 Tall Purple Fleabane
Erigeron peregrinus
Wild Buckwheat
Bistorta bistortoides
(formerly Polygonum bistortoides)
An alpine carpet at nearly 12,000 ft below Hope Lake in the San Juan Mountains, Colorado. The white tufts of buckwheat are also known as Smokeweed and, more simply, as Bistort. Purple Fleabane is also called Mountain Erigeron.

33 Paintbrush
Castilleja rhexifolia
Wild Buckwheat
Bistorta bistortoides
Groundsel
Senecio crassulus
Hope Lake, Colorado. Wildflowers dominate a landscape too harsh, too high, for even the toughest trees. (For more on Paintbrush, see notes for pages 55/61.)

34 Yellow Lady's Slipper
Cypripedium calceolus
A threatened beauty. Never pick this, or any mountain orchid! Almost impossible to find in the southern Rockies, and now alas, quite rare in the northern Rockies too. Loves wet marshy bogs; easiest to find in the Canadian parks: Yoho, Kootenay and Jasper, where they are protected from picking. Blooms in early summer.

36 Fairy Slipper
Calypso bulbosa
The most spectacular of all mountain orchids. This rare prize blooms in deep shady areas beneath dense trees, around mid June. You must look with more than usual attention for these orchids among the debris of the forest floor, as they are only about an inch long. Also called Venus Slipper and Calypso Orchid. Like many orchids it grows in symbiosis with certain fungi, and so can't be transplanted. Don't even try!

37 Mountain Lady's Slipper
Cypripedium montanum
A beautiful and slightly larger relative of the Yellow Lady's Slipper. The White Slipper is always framed by three spiraling darkish sepals. May, June. Easier to find in the Canadian Rockies than in the US.

38 Spotted Orchid
Orchis rotundifolia
These are the tiniest of the mountain orchids. You have to lie down on the ground next to them to appreciate the strange beauty of their doll-like blossoms. Wet ground, early in the season. Also called Round Leaved Orchid.

39 Shooting Star
Dodecatheon pulchellum
The adjective *pulchellum* means "beautiful," which in a non-botanical sense applies to all Shooting Stars. Meadow dwellers, tiny, close to the ground, early summer.

40 Twin Flowers
Linnaea borealis
These paired white blossoms grow in miniature "groves" on stalks 5 to 10 cm. high. They're named after Carl Linnaeus, the Swedish botanist who created modern botanical nomenclature. Found around the world in northern latitudes.

41 Dwarf Dogwood
Chamaepericlymenum canadense
(formerly Cornus canadensis)
Another beauty of the forest floor; produces clusters of vivid red berries in fall, hence its other name of Bunchberry. Likes the rotting wood and deep shade of montane forests in the northern Rockies.

42 Yellow Columbine
43
45 *Aquilegia flavescens*
This flower seems as ubiquitous, and as symbolic a part of the landscape in the northern Rockies as the Blue Columbine is in the southern Rocky Mountains. It too grows on exposed rocky slopes above timberline and, to the special delight of hikers, tends to bloom in profusion at trailside.

46 Shortstyle Wild Onion
47 *Allium brevistylum*
Formerly a part of the diet of many Indian tribes; praised by Lewis and Clark; today eaten only by bear, elk, deer and the like. Flowers all summer long, almost to timberline.

48 Skyrocket
49 *Ipomopsis aggregata*
Tall One-sided Penstemon
Penstemon unilateralis
A midsummer tapestry, Turkey Creek Mesa, San Juan Mountains, Colorado. Skyrocket is also called Scarlet Gilia and, by old timers in Colorado mining camps, Fairy Trumpet. Found throughout the Rockies, generally red/scarlet but occasionally pink or even white.

50 Orange Sneezeweed
Dugaldia hoopesii
Arnica
Arnica sp.
Paintbrush
Castilleja sp.
Wild Buckwheat
Bistorta bistortoides
Sticky Geranium
Geranium richardsonii

51 Fireweed
52 *Chamerion platyphyllum*
53 *(formerly Epilobium angustifolium)*
What a misnomer, nothing about this stately flower resembles a weed! But the first half of its name is explained by Fireweed's tendency to colonize burnt and disturbed land. Young plants make good eating in salads, and the flowers themselves seem to be popular snacks for deer. Fireweed becomes more spectacular, and grows taller, the farther north one goes, reaching shoulder height in the Yukon and Alaska.

54 Blue Columbine
Aquilegia coerulea
The Colorado State Flower. Primarily a southern Rockies species. Still common today but less abundant than at the turn of the century due to overpicking. (In one sense, any picking of wildflowers is overpicking.) Now protected by law. Grows tenaciously in high boulderfields and meadows above timberline, as well as in open forests and meadows of the subalpine zone.

55 Blue Columbine
Aquilegia coerulea
Giant Red Paintbrush
Castilleja miniata
Paintbrush are a delight and a headache. They hybridize so readily, it seems, that one can never quite rely on one's field guide to identify precisely any particular example.

56 Paintbrush
Castilleja sp.
Intensity and diversity of color rather than the form of individual Paintbrush constitute this flower's main charm, at least to me. But it's interesting that the petals aren't brightly colored at all. The bright crimson parts are so-called "floral bracts," a leaflike structure which surrounds the mostly green petals.

58 Giant Red Paintbrush
Castilleja miniata

59 Paintbrush
Castilleja sp.
Wild Chives
Allium schoenoprasum
Wild chives are delicious flowers in every sense. Since they grow like weeds in moist mountain meadows, there's no harm in picking a couple to flavor a camp meal. Also called Purple Onion.

60 Desert Paintbrush
Castilleja chromosa
Most species of Paintbrush that flourish in the arid zones on the western slope of the Rockies seem to be more spikey, less graceful of form, than their high-mountain cousins. But their colors are, if anything, more shocking and brilliant.

61 Lemon Paintbrush
Castilleja occidentalis
Although yellow paintbrush are found throughout the subalpine zone and even lower, they really dazzle the eye in high open meadows of the alpine zone above timberline. Also called Sulphur Paintbrush.

62 Yellow Monkey Flower
Mimulus guttatus
A member of the same Figwort family as the Paintbrush, these flowers flourish in damp wet places and are sometimes known as Seep Spring Monkey Flower. *Guttatus* is Latin for speckled, and refers to tiny crimson spots that dot the snapdragonlike tongue of the flower. Blooms all summer.

63 Elephant's Head
Pedicularis groenlandica
Yet another Figwort cousin of the Paintbrush. A closeup look at this spikey little flower rewards you with a vision of pink elephant's heads complete with gracefully curved trunks, stacked one on top of the other like some primitive natural model for a totem pole. Standing above these small flowers, which grow in large masses across wet meadows, one can't really make out their unusual shape. From a few inches away, they're fantastic. Blooms from June on.

64 Orange Sneezeweed
Dugaldia hoopesii
(formerly Helenium hoopesii)
Sticky Geranium
Geranium richardsonii
A floral carpet in Gold King Basin, a deserted gold mining venue in southwestern Colorado. Orange Sneezeweed is a cheerfully ragged "sunflower" sort of blossom, brightening mountain meadows in the southern Rockies: New Mexico, Colorado, and parts of Wyoming.

66 Mountain Harebell
Campanula rotundifolia
Butter and Eggs
Linaria vulgaris
Butter and Eggs, or Common Toadflax, is half wildflower, half tameflower — gracing gardens in almost all Rocky Mountain towns, as well as prospering in the same sort of inhospitable and disturbed soil as Mountain Harebell. A common beauty.

67 Mountain Harebell
Campanula rotundifolia
Mountain Harebell flourishes on sunny rocky slopes (including road cuts) along the entire length of the Rockies. The name Harebell is thought to be a reference to witches who could turn themselves into hares, and indeed this particular Bluebell is sometimes called Witches' Thimble. Flowers all summer.

68 Mariposa Lily
69 *Calochortus gunnisonii*
An eyedazzler. (Mariposa is Spanish for butterfly.) Flowers through July in open fields. One of the silliest things that can be said about this wildflower is that it's edible (apparently Indians taught Mormon settlers to eat the virtually identical Sego Lily, *Calochortus nuttallii*, in times of famine). You'd feel like a cannibal to eat such a beauty.

70 Butterweed Groundsel
Senecio serra
Midsummer Teton gold. Butterweed Groundsel is common throughout the Yellowstone/Grand Teton area, coloring the high sagebrush flats long after most other summer flowers have shriveled up.

71 Mule's Ears
Wyethia amplexicaulis
See notes for pages 14 & 15.

73 Colorado Loco
Oxytropis lambertii
Tall One Sided Penstemon
Penstemon unilateralis
Paintbrush
Castilleja sp.
A pointillist patchwork of purple, orange and magenta, Specie Mesa, Colorado. Colorado Loco (also called Lambert's Loco or Purple Loco) is one of the infamous western loco weeds that really does drive grazing animals crazy and can even kill them. Found, as here, in open fields and meadows.

74 Shortstyle Wild Onion
Allium brevistylum
Mountain Meadow Cinquefoil
Potentilla diversifolia
Midsummer meadow, central Wyoming. (See notes for pages 46/47.)

75 Paintbrush, Cinquefoil, Sticky Geranium & Sedges
A tricolor tapestry, Elk Range, Colorado.

76 Green Gentian
Frasera speciosa
The Green Gentian, standing waist to head tall, is an alpine monster. It's also aptly called Monument Plant — for its imposing size — and sometimes, Deer's Ears or Deer Tongue. Walk up for a close inspection of its surrealistic flowers which are not very evident, even from a few feet away. Blooms on open hillsides all the way up to timberline.

77 Big Mountain Gentian
Pneumonanthe parryi
One of the most classic, most loved, of all Alpine flowers. An almost identical Gentian is enshrined in the Alpine folklore of Austria, Switzerland and France, much like the famous Edelweiss. But unlike this latter, the exquisite Blue Gentian flourishes all over the Rockies from Colorado to Canada. Also called Explorer's Gentian, Blue Gentian and Pleated Gentian. Found both below and far above timberline.

78 Bear Grass
Xerophyllum tenax
Paintbrush
Castilleja sp.
Tall Purple Fleabane
Erigeron peregrinus
Bear Grass is a northern Rockies phenomenon that looks as if it comes from another planet. These tall, white, candlelike flowers on slender stalks abound on open hillsides and alpine meadows in Idaho, Montana and just across the border in Waterton Lakes National Park, Canada. Individual plants only bloom every few years. Also known as Indian Basket Grass, Squaw Grass, Elk Grass, Turkey Beard, Bear Lily, and Pine Lily. (They are, indeed, members of the Lily family.) Mountainsides of Bear Grass are an unforgettable spectacle.

79 Chainpod
Hedysarum boreale
A beautiful pea-like foothill flower, fairly common in Montana.

81 Sky Pilot
Polemonium viscosum
Highest of the high tundra flowers of the Rockies, this funnel or trumpet shaped flower can be found on the actual summits of some 14,000 ft. peaks in Colorado. Its leaves give off an offensive odor if crushed, but it grows in such high remote locations, and contrasts so strongly with its rocky environment, that there's no danger of stepping on it and crushing it.

82 Spotted Saxifrage
Ciliaria austromontana
(formerly Saxifraga bronchialis)
A high-altitude mat of mossy green with a haze of tiny star-shaped flowers a few inches above it. The name Saxifrage comes from the Latin for break/rock. This charming flower doesn't break rocks but lives, instead, in breaks, cracks and ledges of rock, rather than in open tundra.

83 Pink Moss Campion
Silene acaulis
Whiplash Saxifrage
Hirculus platysepalus
A high-tundra adaptation par excellence, Moss Campion is a circumpolar plant that hugs the ground to shed wind. Also called Moss Pink, it spreads in a cushion or pillow across stony, gravely soil. A mid to late summer bloomer, depending on altitude and exposure. The tiny yellow flowers are Whiplash Saxifrage.

84 Spring Beauty
Claytonia megarhiza
Dwarf Clover
Trifolium nanum
Pussy Toes
Antennaria sp.
Spring Beauty is the most startling flower on Rocky Mountain tundra for the geometric perfection of its circle of white blossoms. Occasionally found over 14,000 ft. Its low circular form is thought to be the most efficient shape for coping with extreme elements; and its single root can penetrate as deep as two meters beneath the inhospitable tundra surface.

85 Dwarf Clover
Trifolium nanum
This hyperadapted member of the pea family is all flower, no stem. It contributes a vivid splash of red to an often monochrome tundra environment.

86 Blue Columbine
Aquilegia coerulea
Primus inter pares, the Blue Columbine dominates the incredible flowerscape of Yankee Boy Basin in the San Juan Mountains of southwest Colorado. Yankee Boy contains the single most impressive collection of showy wildflowers in one mountain valley that we have ever seen. It's a site that deserves and needs protection. Why not a National Wildflower Preserve?

87 Paintbrush
Castilleju rhexifolia & sp.
Queen Anne's Lace
Daucus carota
It's hard to believe that delicate white sunbursts of Queen Anne's Lace are actually the antecedents of our everyday carrots, but so it is. Yankee Boy Basin, Colorado.

89 Blue Columbine
Aquilegia coerulea
Yankee Boy Basin, Colorado.

Note: The botanical names in these notes follow the treatment in Weber, 1987, confirmed by Katharine I. Matthews.

About the photographs:
These images were all produced with Nikon cameras and lenses. Naturally, for wildflower photography the workhorse is a close-up or macro lens (Nikon calls it a "micro" lens). Mine is a 55mm f2.8, and I never go out without it. But actually I use my entire range of lenses for wildflower photography, from 300mm to 18mm, often with extension tubes. To get right next to certain individual beauties, I prefer a tripod that lowers all the way down to ground level with a ball-and-socket head.
   In recent years I've switched to Fujichrome 50 film. At present Fujichrome seems to be the state of the art emulsion for rich, saturated colors. All the pictures in this book were taken in available light without flash.

Wildflower Source List:
There are numerous wildflower books and field guides. Some are scholarly and authoritative, but assume a fair amount of botanical sophistication. Others are simplified popular guides, arranged by the color of the flowers, and can be wonderful helpers as you begin your own wildflower adventures. The following list contains a good cross section:

Craighead, John J. & Frank C. Craighead. *A Field Guide to Rocky Mountain Wildflowers.* Houghton Mifflin, 1963.

Nelson, Ruth Ashton. *Handbook of Rocky Mountain Plants.* Skyland Publishers, 1979.

Porsild, A. E. *Rocky Mountain Wildflowers.* National Museum of Natural Sciences, National Museums of Canada, 1979.

Scotter, George W. & Hälle Flygare. *Wildflowers of the Canadian Rockies.* Hurtig Publishers, 1986.

Shaw, Richard J. *Plants of Yellowstone and Grand Teton National Parks.* Wheelwright Press, 1981.

Spellenberg, Richard. *The Audubon Society Field Guide to North American Wildflowers, Western Region.* Alfred Knopf, 1979

Weber, William A. *Rocky Mountain Flora: Western Slope.* Colorado Associated University Press, 1987 (in press).

HIGH COLOR
Spectacular Wildflowers of the Rockies
is published by Western Eye Press
Box 917, Telluride, Colorado 81435.

Photographs copyright © 1987
by Linde Waidhofer.
Text copyright © 1987
by Lito Tejada-Flores.

ISBN 0-941283-00-3
Library of Congress Catalogue Number:
86-51480.

The text of High Color is set in Palatino,
a modern classic designed by Herman Zapf;
the display type is ITC Eras, designed by
Albert Boton.
Typography by Ed Nies of Mel Typesetting,
on a Macintosh driven Linotronic 300.
Book design by Lito Tejada-Flores.
Production coordination by Tommy Lee.

Printed in Hong Kong by Pacific Rim
International Printing.

Special thanks to Katharine Matthews,
friend, botanist and specialist in alpine
plants, who was kind enough to review the
wildflower notes for accuracy and update our
identifications.

Original, signed, handmade photographic
prints of the illustrations in this book are
available from Linde Waidhofer through
Western Eye Press. For details and prices,
write to:
High Color Portfolio
Western Eye Press
Box 917, Telluride, Colorado 81435